This book is dedicated to *Blue Peter* viewers, Tony of *East 17* and Born Free supporters everywhere.

Published in the United States in 1998 by The Millbrook Press, Inc., 2 Old New Milford Road, Brookfield, CT 0680⁴

A TEMPLAR BOOK
Devised and produced by The Templar Company plc, Pippbrook Mill, London Road, Dorking, Surrey RH4 1JE, in association with The Born Free Foundation.

Library of Congress Cataloging-in-Publication Data
Travers, Will.
The elephant truck / written by Will Travers ; illustrated by Lawrie Taylor.
p.      cm.  —  (Born free wildlife books)
"A Templar book."
Summary: Tells the story of Tembo, the first elephant to be relocated in a program to move elephants to safer, less populated areas in Kenya. Includes a section with facts and photographs about Kenya's Elephant Translocation Programme and the work of the Born Free Foundation.
ISBN 0-7613-0408-8 (lib. bdg.)
1. African elephant—Juvenile fiction. [1. African elephant—Fiction. 2. Elephants—Fiction. 3. Wildlife rescue—Fiction. 4. Kenya—Fiction.} I. Taylor, Lawrie, ill. II. Title. III. Series
PZ10.3.T7565E1  1988
[Fic]—dc21                               97-34230
                                            CIP
                                             AC
Edited by AJ.Wood and Dugald Steer. Designed by Mike Jolley.
This book has been printed and bound in Belgium using 100% recycled paper.
No dioxin-producing chlorine is used in the manufacturing process.

WRITTEN BY *Will Travers*

# the Elephant truck

ILLUSTRATED BY *Lawrie Taylor*

The world's human population is growing at an alarming rate. There are six billion people alive on our planet today and this figure will probably rise to ten billion or more in the next sixty years. How will wildlife be able to live in a world so full of people?

One answer lies in the setting up of national parks. In these places, wild animals come first. For Kenya's elephants, such parks offer a ray of hope, particularly for those animals living in small areas of wilderness surrounded by a sea of humanity.

As farmers try to protect their crops from hungry elephants, and the elephants follow their natural desire to find food, there is a growing danger that either humans or animals will get hurt or even killed. Kenya's Elephant Translocation Program is designed to help solve this problem, and everyone at the Born Free Foundation is honored to have been a part of its launch. We hope that you enjoy reading the story of that launch and how we moved the first elephant to safety. We hope that many more elephants will follow, and that the project will succeed, saving both human and animal lives.

WILL TRAVERS
*The Born Free Foundation*

*The Elephant Truck*

Deep in the thick, thorny bush the elephants paused. The three animals stood, flapping their great ears, listening intently. Far away they could hear a strange sound, different from the buzz of flies and the other familiar noises of the African bush. This was a deeper, more regular staccato drone that seemed to come from high overhead. As the noise came closer, the elephants moved further into the thickets, nervous and afraid, until at last it whirred away, disappearing into the distance.

*The Elephant Truck*

The elephants had heard the sound before. They had even seen its source – a shiny machine that swooped and hung in the sky, floating above them like some gigantic bird of prey. It made them feel afraid.

They had become used to feeling that way—ever since the day when they had first stumbled hungrily from the edges of their sun-parched wilderness, delighted to find the strange fields of corn and millet spread out before them. In the dry season when food was so scarce here suddenly was a seemingly endless supply...

At that very first feast groups of men had come to try and scare them away, but hunger made the elephants brave. They had been to the fields again last night, but the men had been waiting for them, beating sheets of metal, letting off firecrackers and shouting angrily.

Tembo, the eldest of the three elephants, understood and feared men. When he was still young, grazing happily with his family, a group of men had come in a four-wheeled machine that crashed and bumped after them. They had fled, but the machine could travel as fast as them and faster.

When the men finally left them alone, Tembo had tried to find his mother amongst the other elephants, but she wasn't there. They had come across her later that day, lying dead and bloody by the tracks of the strange machine. Her tusks had been taken, sawn roughly from the great bulk of her body. That was what men could do.

But despite his fear, Tembo still raided the farmers' fields, his hunger spurring him on. With each visit, he sensed the mens' anger growing. Soon more blood would be spilt, but would it be man's or elephant's?

*The Elephant Truck*

Now Tembo shuffled nervously in the thicket as the droning sound returned and the shiny machine appeared again, bursting into view over the top of the nearest clump of trees. Startled, the elephants lifted their trunks in alarm, trying to sense from which direction the danger would come. Tembo led the others up the hill, but the machine stayed with them. It came even lower and the elephants broke into a run. Tembo only managed ten or twelve paces before he heard a short, loud crack and felt a sharp sting pierce his rump. He continued to run, but suddenly his legs wobbled and buckled beneath him. His two companions trumpeted in alarm and fled as Tembo fell heavily to the ground.

*The Elephant Truck*

It was strange and frightening.
Tembo found that he could hear and see,
but he could not move at all. He felt dazed, gripped
by a terrible panic. He wanted to get up and run away, but he
could do nothing but remain still, lying silently in the dust.
Then he heard the sound of men. Here they came, shouting
to each other, running toward him. Tembo had a sudden
vision of his mother. Was his fate
to be the same?

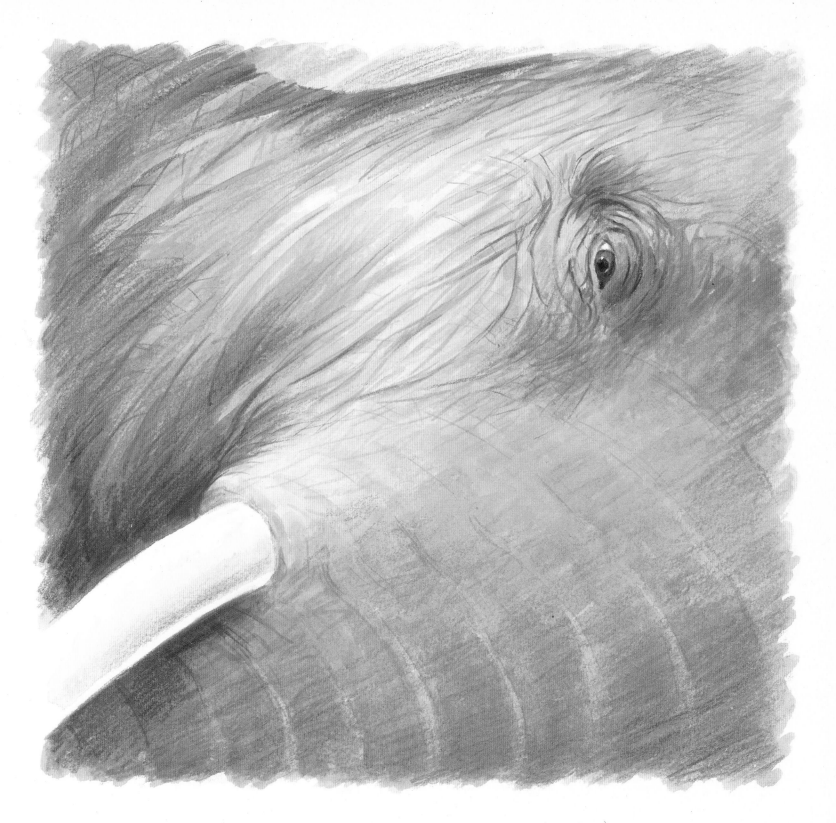

*The Elephant Truck*

The men gathered around him and the air was filled with their jabbering talk. One of them came close, gently holding the edge of his ear, and looked him straight in the eye. Tembo wanted to swipe him away, but his trunk lay on the ground, feeble and still.

Moments later another sound came roaring and crashing through the bush. It was a machine like the one that had chased him long ago, only bigger. It was full of men and, with a hiss, a whirr, and a screech, the machine seemed to split in half and a massive box swung off its back onto the ground next to him.

*The Elephant Truck*

By now more men had arrived. One of them shone a bright light into his eyes. "We'll have to hurry," he called to the others. Tembo was puzzled. These men didn't seem angry like the men in the fields. Working quickly, they eased a strap around his neck and fixed ropes to his feet. They were tipping him over!

Tembo's world turned upside down as the men pulled him onto a flat metal tray. "We've got the radio collar on," cried the man with the light. "Pull him in!"

Tembo felt the earth sliding under him as he was hauled into the darkness of the wooden box. The men untied the ropes from around his feet and then, with a massive thud, they closed the doors behind him. Everything went quiet. Outside, Tembo could sense the men waiting, silent and anxious.

Then a small door opened at the back of the box and a man climbed in. He bent over Tembo, and the elephant felt another sharp sting behind his ear. As the man slipped away, Tembo felt a trembling in his legs and then, suddenly, his strength came flooding back. He struggled to his feet with surprise and let out a low rumble.

*The Elephant Truck*

Tembo stamped his feet. He waved his trunk. Then he began to push against the sides of the crate, but the box held firm. He could not walk forward or backward—on every side, the walls hemmed him in.

A fresh wave of fear ran through him as he felt the box jerk violently upward. It swung slowly to and fro before it was eased gently down onto the back of the truck.

*The Elephant Truck*

All around him, Tembo could hear the men cheering as the machine roared to life and began to move off, gaining speed as it rumbled heavily through the undergrowth.

Branches ripped and clattered against the side of the box as the truck rolled on and on through the bush. It was taking him away from the land that was his home, that was for sure, but why and where to? Tembo had no idea at all.

Above him, through the wire roof, Tembo could see the night sky. He had watched as the daylight had faded and now a bright moon hovered above him. The smells of the bush had been replaced by other, stranger scents – burning wood and burning maize, the smell and noise of many people, acrid, chemical, unnatural smells. The sound of machines filled the air and the sky was colored a strange electric white which blocked out the stars.

He could hear the voices of the men who were driving the truck. "Nairobi!" one of them shouted. "We're halfway there."
If there was meaning to the words, Tembo could not understand them. Yet he understood that the men were excited, as though something they wanted was gradually being accomplished.
Then the sounds and smells of the strange land receded and, as the truck rolled on through the velvety night, Tembo began to doze.

*The Elephant Truck*

Tembo awoke with the slowing of the truck and he noticed that it was morning. The roar of the engine shuddered and died. The air was still. Strange and wonderful scents filtered in to greet him – it had rained recently and there was a smell of wet earth, mixed with the perfume of wild flowers.

Tembo was confused. What did these men want with him? Why had they brought him to this new wilderness, that was at once so familiar and at the same time so different from the land that was his home?

Tembo stood very still inside the box.

He heard the sound of feet climbing up outside.

"OK! PULL!" he heard a voice shout. Then a miracle happened.

The door began to swing open. At first Tembo thought it was another trap.

Perhaps he would feel another sharp sting in his back.

Perhaps his legs would buckle beneath him again.

So he just stood still and waited.

$N$ow the door was fully open. Through it Tembo could see hills and trees, earth and grass. He stepped out slowly and then, from the corner of his eye, he saw the men watching him. Some of them were smiling, as if they'd achieved something that had made them happy. But Tembo could not understand why. His anger exploded and he charged toward them.

With pleasure he saw the humans dive and scramble for cover. Then he spun away in a cloud of dust and moved quickly up the hillside, out of sight.

To his surprise, no one came after him.
He understood then that the men had brought him here
and now they had set him free. As he stood alone in this new
country he began to smell the presence of other elephants.
They were strangers to him, but they were his own kind.
With a shake of his mighty head he strode forward
to find them, free at last!

The elephant-damaged fields and grain stores on the edge of the Mwea Reserve.

On the other side of Kenya, the wild expanses of Tsavo National Park provide a safe haven for Africa's native animals.

All over Africa elephants are in danger. Most people have heard stories of elephants killed for the magnificent ivory of their tusks. But many face another, less obvious danger, born of the endless conflict between the growing needs of the human world and that of the planet's wildlife.

# Addendum
## THE **REAL** STORY

"More than any other animal the elephant symbolizes the spirit and soul of Africa."

*Will Travers, The Born Free Foundation*

Partly, the conflict stems from nature itself, from the vicious yearly cycle that often leaves elephants without food, surrounded by a drought-ridden wilderness. Set alongside this the continual spread of humanity – the constant need for people to claim new land, using technology to help them grow food and raise families, even in the most arid conditions – and you begin to see the problem.

Mwea National Reserve, just over 25 square miles (40 kilometers) of bush bordered by local farms and lakes, is home to 47 elephants as well as countless other animals. Each elephant can eat up to 660 pounds of food a day and, during the dry season, such food is often hard to come by. Tempted by the nearby fields, full of succulent crops, it's hardly surprising that the elephants leave the reserve and help themselves. Neither is it surprising that the local farmers try to protect their crops, anxious that otherwise their families will go hungry. In such a situation it's easy to see how both elephants and people can get hurt or even killed. So what can be done to safeguard both their futures?

## Operation Tembo is Born

The President of Kenya and Dr. David Western, Director of the Kenya Wildlife Service, decided that one answer to the problem would be to transport the elephants from small reserves like Mwea to the wide expanses of Tsavo National Park in the southeast of the country. There, they would have enough space and food to live without the need to stray outside. But how could such a move be achieved?

Elephants take a drink at a Tsavo waterhole.

Our Elephant Translocation Truck being loaded up, ready for its journey to Africa.

Children from a village bordering Mwea — crop damage by elephants may mean that they go hungry.

Stuart Miles from BBC's Blue Peter examines the damage done to a farmer's crop stores after a nighttime raid by elephants.

East 17 arrives at Mwea.

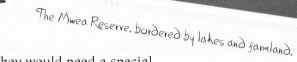

The Mwea Reserve, bordered by lakes and farmland.

They would need a special vehicle to move a creature as large and powerful as an elephant. They would need experts on hand to ensure the animals' safety. And most of all they would need money. Luckily, the Born Free Foundation was on hand to help. This is how we helped Operation Tembo to become a reality.

## April 1995

After discussions with Dr. Western and the Kenyan government, the Born Free Foundation launches its campaign to raise money for Operation Tembo.

Through an appeal on the BBC's *Blue Peter* program, and thanks to the generosity of countless people, they raise £100,000 (about $160,000) in only eight weeks.

## July 1995

The money is used to design and purchase the most advanced animal transport vehicle in Africa. Known affectionately as East 17 because of the large donation made by pop group *East 17*'s singer/songwriter Tony Mortimer, this

Elephant Translocation Truck has ten wheels and powerful cranes capable of lifting more than eighteen tons. At last, Operation Tembo is ready to roll.

## September 1996 – Friday the 29th

The Operation Tembo team gather at Mwea National Reserve, 56 miles (90 kilometers) southeast of Mount Kenya. Present are experts from the Kenya Wildlife Service, consultants from Zimbabwe, Stuart Miles and the *Blue Peter* crew, and myself. Meanwhile, 93 miles (150 kilometers) away, the East 17 truck, with designer George Drake at the wheel, leaves Nairobi on the first stage of its mission.

## Saturday the 30th

While the rest of the team make preparations, Stuart and I take a short safari through the Mwea Reserve, witnessing the effects of elephants on the local vegetation and talking to local farmers about the problems they face coexisting with the elephants that frequently raid their crops.

That evening we join George Drake, world-famous elephant expert Clem Coetzee, Dr. John Waithaka from the KWS and vet Richard Kock as final tests are carried out on the truck in readiness for the following day.

## October 1996 – Sunday the 1st

Very early the next morning the team leaves the camp and assembles on one of the dirt roads that cut through the Mwea Reserve. Dr. Kock and Clem set off in a helicopter

Above, vet Dr. Richard Kock prepares the immobilising dart for the helicopter crew.

Left, Richard radios the support team.

Below, the team on the ground fit a radio collar to the sedated Tembo.

The carrying box is lowered to the ground, ready to load Tembo.

A final check-up from the vets...

to find and select the first elephant to be moved.

After a frustrating morning of attempts to find a suitable animal, a bull—Tembo—is located and shot with a dart loaded with a tranquilizer.

A clearing is made around the immobilized body of Tembo and George moves East 17 into position. Dr. Kock and his team check to see that Tembo's breathing and heartbeat are normal and attach a radio control collar around his neck so that they can follow his movements after the translocation. The 8-ton carrying box is unloaded and our crew of forty men manage to roll all 11,000 pounds (5,000 kilos) of Tembo onto a pallet before sliding him into the box. The antidote to the tranquilizer is administered and we are all relieved to see that Tembo is standing upright in the box. George starts the truck and our convoy sets off through the bush.

## Monday 2nd

We drive through the night, 310 miles (500 kilometers) across Kenya to Tsavo National Park. I discover during the journey

...And Tembo is rolled onto the metal pallet.

that Tsavo National Park was set up in 1948—12,427 square miles (20,000 square kilometers) of unspoiled Kenyan bush, the largest national park in Africa. David Western flies in to meet us and to advise everyone of the chosen release sight.

During the whole process, the veterinary team keep a constant check on Tembo's condition and help to keep him cool with regular splashes of water.

As the sun sets, the carrying box is lifted back up onto East 17. We're ready to roll!

At last we reach Tsavo! The convoy, with its precious cargo, heads for the release site on the Yatta Plateau.

The convoy rolls on through the red dust, deep into the heart of Tsavo. We cross the Tsavo River at Lugards Falls and head up onto the remote Yatta Plateau. It is here that Tembo will finally be given his freedom.

After careful assessment of his health, the doors of the box are opened and Tembo steps gingerly outside. With amazing speed he charges at us, stopping just short in a cloud of dust. Seconds later, he has disappeared out of sight.

We all breath a huge sigh of relief. The first stage in Kenya's elephant translocation project is safely over. There are many more elephants to move but at least we can look forward with confidence now that our first attempt has been successful – Tembo is now in his new home, none the worse for his epic journey. Everyone, including Clem Coetzee the wildlife expert who has probably helped move more elephants than anyone else in the world, is smiling!

Tembo charges the release team before heading for the hills, free to explore his new home.

● An elephant's trunk contains nearly 100,000 muscles. They are used for lifting objects of all sizes, and also to greet other elephants in a 'trunk touch.' Elephants can use their trunks as snorkels, to breathe underwater or in deep mud.

● In the period from 1979-1989, the elephant population almost halved, with up to 300 elephants being killed each day, as the value of ivory reached $90 a pound. By the late 1980s many of the mature breeding males had been wiped out.

● A cow elephant's pregnancy lasts 22 months—compared to 9 months for a human. When born, an elephant weighs about 264 pounds (120 kilograms), which is more than most fully grown human beings. Elephant calves suckle for about two years.

● Elephants are vegetarian and need to eat up to 500 pounds (250 kilograms) of food every day. They eat leaves, grass, twigs and small branches. If a herd of elephants is forced to live in a small area, they will devastate the habitat.

● Elephants can live up to 60 or 70 years in the wild.

● The elephant has six sets of teeth, compared to our two, but they only use one set at a time. Each set is made of two teeth on the top jaw and two on the bottom. These teeth move forward as they wear out, and are replaced by the next set.

# HOW TO TELL THE DIFFERENCE BETWEEN AN AFRICAN AND ASIAN ELEPHANT.

## WEIGHT AND HEIGHT

Asian elephants are smaller, weigh about 8,800 pounds (4,000 kilograms) and stand about 10 feet (3 meters) at the shoulder. African elephants weigh about 13,200 pounds (6,000 kilograms) and stand about 12 feet (3.5 meters) tall.

## TUSKS

Both male and female African elephants have tusks. In Asian elephants only the males have tusks and they are generally smaller.

## EARS

African elephants' ears are much larger. African elephants ears are the shape of Africa, Asian elephants ears are the shape of India.